How to Draw
FARM ANIMALS

How to Draw
FARM ANIMALS

Barbara Soloff Levy

DOVER PUBLICATIONS, INC.
Mineola, New York

Bibliographical Note

How to Draw Farm Animals is a new work, first published by Dover
Publications, Inc., in 2006.

International Standard Book Number

ISBN-13: 978-0-486-47200-3
ISBN-10: 0-486-47200-0

Manufactured in the United States by Courier Corporation
47200003   2014
www.doverpublications.com

Note

A farm is a very busy place! In this book you will learn how to draw pictures of some of the people, animals, buildings, and tools you might find on a working farm.

There are four steps to each drawing. Start with the simplest step at the top left part of the page. Then do the step to the right, followed by the step on the bottom left and the step at the bottom right. You may want to trace the steps first, just to get a feel for drawing. Use a pencil in case you need to make changes along the way. There's also a Practice Page opposite each drawing page for you to use.

When you are pleased with your drawing, you can go over the lines with a felt-tip pen or colored pencil. Erase the dotted lines when you get to the last step. Finally, you can color in your drawings any way you wish. After you have finished all thirty drawings, why don't you try to make up some drawings of your own? Have fun, and enjoy your visit to a farm!

2   Farmer Bob

Practice Page

Practice Page

6   Barn and Silo

8   Tractor

Practice Page

10   Cat

Practice Page

12   Goose

Practice Page

Practice Page

Practice Page

18   Cow

Practice Page

20   Hen

Practice Page

22   Chick

Practice Page

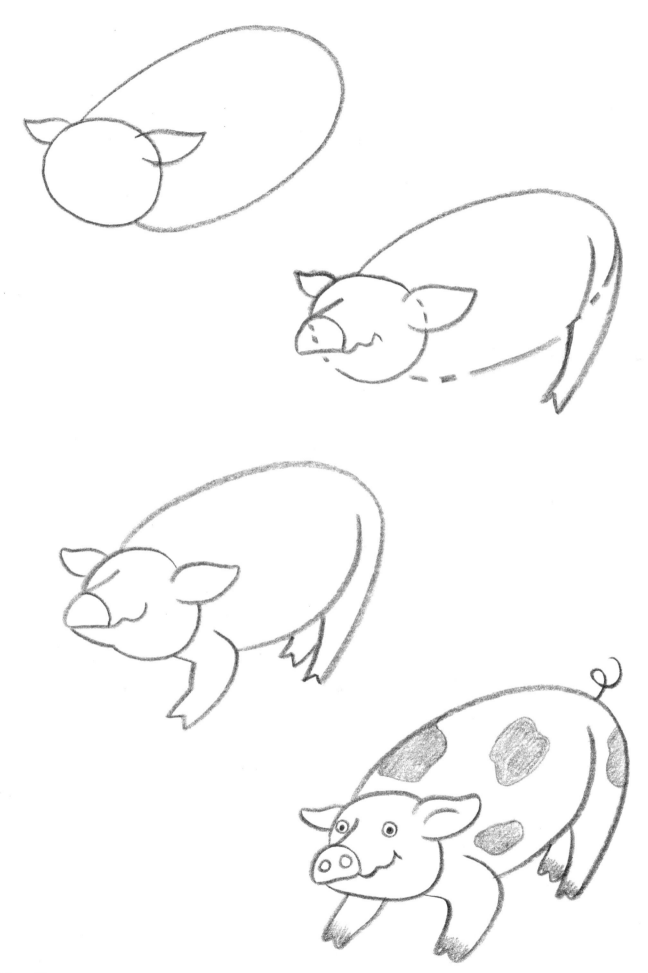

Practice Page

26   Horse

Practice Page

28   Barn Owl

Practice Page

30 Goat

Practice Page

34   Rabbit

Practice Page

Practice Page

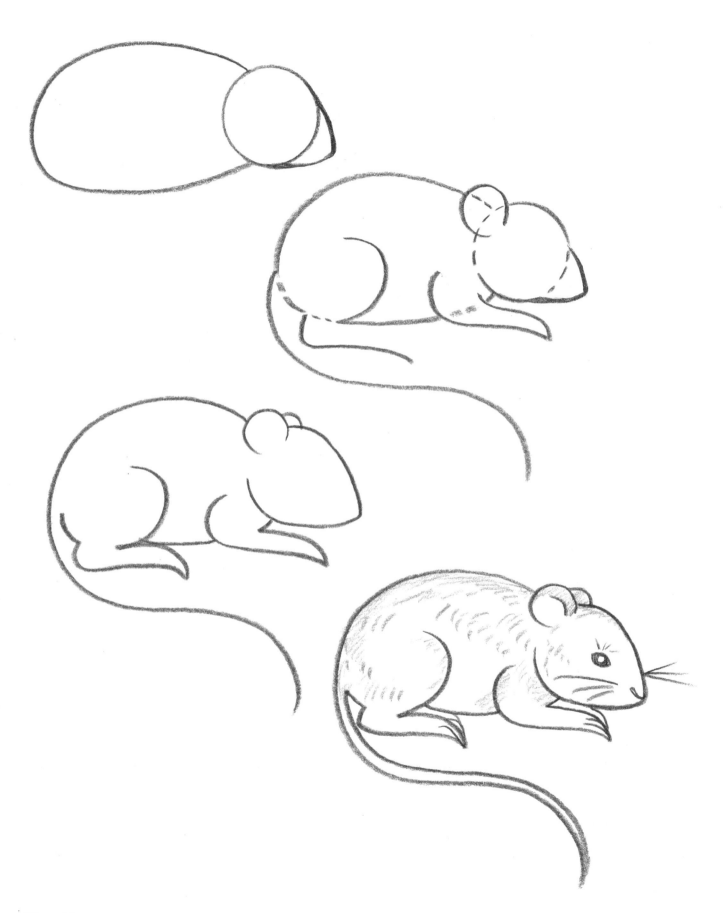

40   Mouse

Practice Page

42   Swallow

44   Swan

Practice Page

46 Bull

Practice Page

48   Donkey

Practice Page

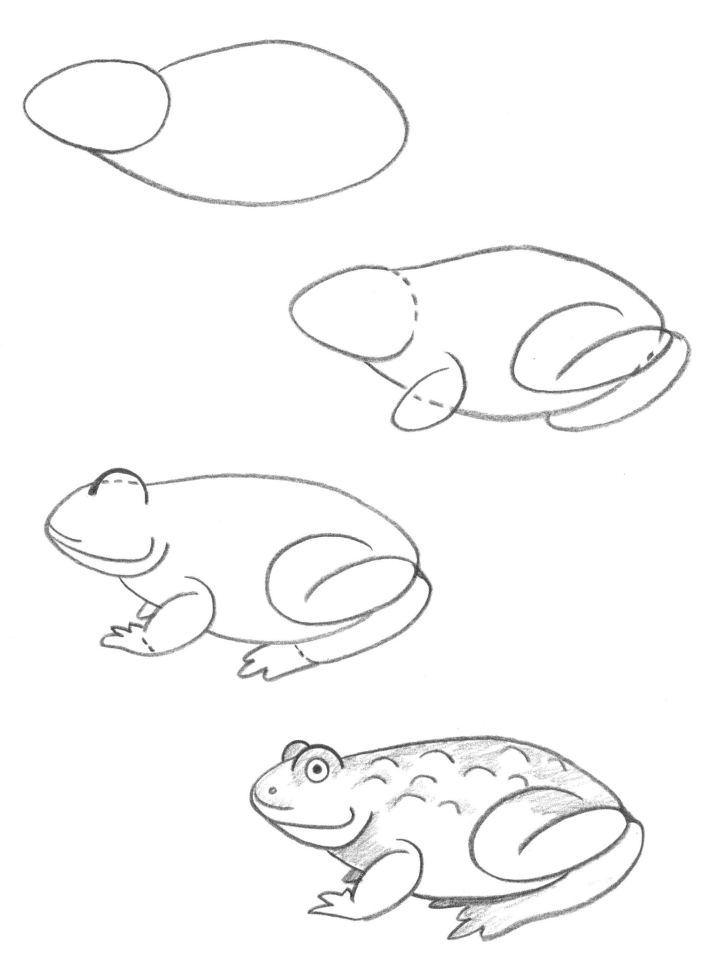

Practice Page

52   Old English Sheepdog

Practice Page

54   Ostrich

Practice Page

56   Llama

Practice Page

58   Border Collie

Practice Page

60   Ox